EL CERRITO starts quiet and small, with a group of friends wandering around the nondescript bay area suburbs of El Cerrito. And then suddenly it is large, mesmerizing, international: Morocco, Sarajevo, Turkey, Jordan. But this is distinctive not just for its global reach. It is a psychogeography that is also a love story, a narrative. It drew me in and then surprised me, in the best way.

–Juliana Spahr, author of *Fuck You-Aloha-I Love You*

I've lived in this part of California all my life, but I've not lived it, not breathed its lives and deaths, as I have, now that I've read Noor Al-Samarrai's *EL CERRITO*. It is thrilling to find a poet who both accurately exposes the history behind every place she encounters (her foot-noting is a living artery of interactivity), and who constantly infuses the page with the frank immediacy of the daily. She does not use language to layer upon it the emotions she'd like to propose we feel, rather she lets the actual vibrate in its own detail, and I feel what is always a complexity that is more than any performed affect, and that is constantly moving in time. Too may poets make a static artifact of the moment. Instead, Ms. Al-Samarrai exposes the micro-tonalities that are the present as it rests uneasily on all that came before. It is James Baldwin whom I hear echo from the pages of this work, when he tells us: "The past is what makes the present coherent, and the past will remain horrible for exactly as long as we refuse to assess it honestly." To that end, this first book encompasses the personal, historical, environmental, and interrogates conceptions of foreignness and belonging, though nothing is moralized, distanced, or decided. We travel with Al-Samarrai and we feel how we might live awake to our own lives. There are, as well, many instances of language-use that invigorate the intuition, such as "neat-gilled and salivating mushrooms with caps covered in a substance like gathered spit, /single link of deer vertebra, /rain-lush slopes. All the way up the hill we heard the highway." But notice that, even in such moments, we are called back to the presence of what concretizes, what constrains, all of us who live in the flat lands of cities in the throws of late capitalism. I will return to read this work often, and then I will go back out into my city to walk with my eyes re-opened, alert to my pulse of the present. I will return to Ms Al-Samarrai's work because she shows me how to stay in motion. She writes, to my mind, in the lineage of Charles Olson, who demands "always one perception must must must MOVE, INSTANTER, ON ANOTHER!" And under the sign of Italo Calvino, when he explains: "… the function of literature is communication between things that are different… not blunting but even sharpening the differences between them, following the true bent of written language." To achieve this, as Ms.Al-Samarrai does, is, to my mind, literature of the highest order.

–Rusty Morrison, author of *the true keeps calm biding its story*

EL CERRITO
By Noor Al-Samarrai

EL CERRITO is typeset in Granjon, a Garamond variant designed by George W. Jones & named for Robert Granjon — on whose work the italic version of the typeface was modeled — who died "a trembling seventy-seven year-old still cutting marvelous punches for the printing offices of the Vatican and Medici."[†] Titles and notes are set in Futura and other design inspiration was found in Guy Debord & Jorn Asger's 1959 book *Mémoires*.

[†] *The Palaeotypography of the French Renaissance*, Hendrik D.L. Vervliet, 2008

Designed and edited by John Trefry
for Inside the Castle.
Cover art "Untitled" by Nalini Sairsingh

This is a text occupying
the expanded field of literature,
from Inside the Castle.
www.insidethecastle.org

ISBN-10: 0999345931
ISBN-13: 978-0999345931

EL CERRITO

HAIBUN

NOOR AL-SAMARRAI

This book is for, and definitely a product of, everyone who has wandered with me, and pushed me past my own borders. for everyone I have met "in passing" along the way. There are a smattering of friends whom I especially need to thank and send love to for their support, so integral in the creation of this book.

I'm grateful to Anna Vignet, who introduced me to the Wanderer's Union and honed my love for wandering more generally, and to Jefferson Tesla Woods, J. Bryce Hidysmith, and Ben Joeng who were often co-conspirators in these travels.

I must thank Cecil Giscombe, who introduced me to Bashō and whose voice has since been a truth detector in my head.
I am grateful to my teachers Robert Hass, Lyn Hejinian, and Ariana Reines from whom I have continued to learn long past the classroom.

I thank Kouros Alaghband, who opened my eyes to new light forms.
I thank Nalini Sairsingh who has taught me to articulate both with and without language.
I am infinitely grateful to Anthony Dubovsky.

The first iteration of *EL CERRITO* was birthed to the tune of Elton John's Crocodile Rock and Robyn in the pink presence of the wonderful Danni Gorden and Melinda Noack.

I thank Ariana Weckstein who loved the early iterations of this work, and who taught me so much about love.

A big thanks to John Trefry who saw the potential in the little collection I sent his way, who invited me to expand it into a full length book and who saw me through the process with a great balance of patience, wonder, and firmness.

I'm inexpressibly grateful to my brother and sister — Hakam and Teeb — and to my parents, Nahla and Najib.

I thank Patrick Forrester for his generosity, for laying me down a pallet on his floor and granting me the time and space to finish this book in a supportive and gentle environment.

Index of Images

Sutro Storm – Anna Vignet

Sandwich, with a circus descendant's arm – Noor Al-Samarrai

Man of the Mountain – Anthony Dubovsky

Toots – Noor Al-Samarrai

A dream of a cow, passing through – Noor Al-Samarrai

A reincarnation of Emilia Cairo – Noor Al-Samarrai

6 a.m. at the Cemetery – Anna Vignet

Witch in the woods – Noor Al-Samarrai

Olives at the market – Noor Al-Samarrai

Horse passing gas – romantic scale – Kouros Alaghband

RUNMARÖ
118, 122, 126

NEW HAVEN
108

DISPOSING OF THE REMAINS
128

SARAJEVO
148, 150, 152, 174

VIŞEGRAD
176

ISTANBUL

YALOVA
144

136

SELÇUK
140

EPHESUS
142

KONYA
156, 158

BEIRUT
94

AMMAN

MADABA
162

TANGIER
166

RABAT
164

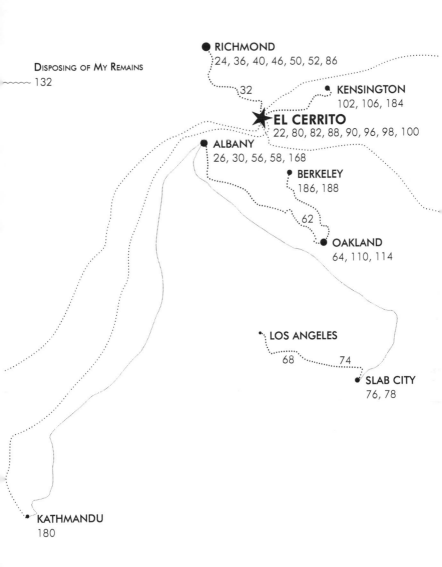

● RICHMOND
24, 36, 40, 46, 50, 52, 86

DISPOSING OF MY REMAINS
~~~ 132

32

● KENSINGTON
102, 106, 184

★ EL CERRITO
22, 80, 82, 88, 90, 96, 98, 100

● ALBANY
26, 30, 56, 58, 168

● BERKELEY
186, 188

62

● OAKLAND
64, 110, 114

● LOS ANGELES
68   74

● SLAB CITY
76, 78

● KATHMANDU
180

"Through Wandering, we can liberate our perception to see the invisible magnificence hidden in plain sight, the incredible variety of being that takes place every day outside our limited frame. One need not travel halfway around the world to experience the pleasure of alienation that accompanies newness."

— The Wanderer's Union[1] (Ian Kizu-Blair, Sam Lavigne, Tyler Nguyen, Jackie Hasa, Yoshi Salaverry, Orion Kellogg)

[1] The Wanderer's Union is a long-distance wandering club with whom anyone can explore the Bay Area.

On March 17, 2012 three friends and I wandered in El Cerrito, California. We also dipped into adjoining sections of Albany and Richmond. We covered about nine miles during four hours of wandering.

I set out to complete the wander alone on December 1, 2012 but it was a blustery, grey day and I felt lonely, so I turned home after only a couple hours and completed the wander with a friend on September 7, 2013.

The notes I took on that first wander in El Cerrito and on subsequent wanders — many far from the alien reaches of home — became this book. Everywhere I go, I think of El Cerrito.

EL CERRITO

OLD WEST GUN ROOM
3509 Carlson Boulevard, El Cerrito, CA 94530

I in rainbow speckle skirt mismatched socks hiking boots and turban
in the gun shop wondered: would you sell me one, Bob?[2] I could blow
the head off a bottle if it's anything like aiming a football – my brother
taught me. That, and tennis balls we plinked on our roof. We broke
a few windows (just like the picture books, blonde boys blushing
sharded shame, mothers admonishing) – and the guilt felt fine.

"Darndest recession
I've ever seen: business
is booming," Bob said.[3]

Duck hunting is particularly popular.

Cardboard cutout Charlton Heston behind him, arms fenders in front
his chest. Flyer by the counter said: Buy a safe for Christmas, get a free
0.25 caliber pistol.

Use your hotplate for a Frisbee.

[2] Robert Weaver is the owner of the Old West Gun Room.

[3] According to the FBI, gun dealers requested a record 1.5 million background checks on potential firearm purchases from the National Instant Criminal Background Check system in December 2011. Nearly half a million of those background checks occurred in the six days preceding Christmas.

99 RANCH SUPERMARKET
3288 Pierce Street #99, Richmond, CA 94804[4]

Hunted for the wine shop we were tasked to find: Red Taste Wine.
It was closed on this Saturday. We four are all too poor to purchase
anything in the grocery store. Patrick said he wanted tea, and the
rest of us realized we did, too, but bought none. We peered in at the
dark behind doors, rows of deep burgundy bottles lining the walls of
bamboo. Munched dumpster bread that Patrick had picked up from
ACME on his way to meet us – cranberry walnut. Everywhere, the
smell of duck.[5]

We left through the parking lot,[6] walking toward Albany Hill. On
Pierce Street, just parallel to Interstate 580[7] – a wall of cement and
sound.[8]

[4] Due to its lack of grocery stores, Richmond, CA has been characterized as a food desert.

[5] "Duck is a popular Asian food. At 99 Ranch you can get dry cured duck, duck wings, duck legs, cooked salted duck eggs and duck feet. Pekin ducks, bred from mallards, are also called Long Island Ducks." Pellissier, Hank. "99 Ranch Market." The New York Times. Published May 21, 2011.

[6] Cerrito Creek runs through part of the parking lot. Friends of Five Creeks, a local community organization dedicated to the area's creeks, criticized mall management for allowing herbicide to spread to the creek area, ravaging native plants there.

[7] While 99 Ranch's address places it in Richmond, it is on the El Cerrito/Richmond border, represented by the Interstate.

[8] Owsley Stanley, the sound technician who created the Grateful Dead's "Wall of Sound" — the first line array speakers ever to be used at concerts — had a methamphetamines lab in Richmond Annex, the neighborhood where 99 Ranch is located. Stanley believed vegetables were toxic, and that breads would cause cancer. He ate a carnivorous diet consisting of meats, cheeses, and other dairy products, including eggs. He ended up dying of throat cancer.

ALBANY HILL[9]

Didn't want wet feet so we wended past – Patrick said, transplanted
Chinese highrises, awkwardly gazing at wee us. To be honest, the
highrises may not have been awkward. They were maybe grand, and
unsettling. Whichever way they were, to wee us, I concede.

Found our way over Cerrito Creek behind cash-torn apartment
buildings. Found a quarter in what I thought was a single-serving
wishing well, finger-deep.

Pon said Ohlone
Crushed acorns[10] there, not only wished on
Franciscan sandstone.

And then found our way up the hill. Surrounded by:

>   Eucalyptus, poison oak,

>   stump sprouting poison oak –

>   Pon reminded me to wash my fingers after
>   untying boots –

>   red tailed hawk   turkey vulture   mallards

orange-peel mushrooms   shelf mushrooms like
fine china growing, neat-gilled and salivating
mushrooms with caps covered in a substance like
gathered spit,

single link of deer vertebra,

rain-lush slopes. All the way up the hill we heard
the highway.

After the Gold Rush,[11] the Judson Powder Works – forced to move
from San Francisco and then out of Berkeley[12] found a new home at
the foot of the hill, then and after rock quarry. To muffle the sound of
accidents at the dynamite factory, the eucalyptus forest was planted.[13]

[9] Before the city of Albany was incorporated, the hill was called "El Cerrito," meaning "little hill." Its indigenous name is unknown.

[10] Oak trees are native to the area, and grow on Albany Hill.

[11] Not riffing off the Neil Young song, although maybe you should put it on right now. Also, *On the Beach*. The whole album, but especially the title track, "Motion Pictures," and "See the Sky about to Rain."

[12] The dynamite factory was forced to move due to consistent accidental explosions.

[13] The Havens Mahogany Eucalyptus & Land Company was a major spur for the presence of eucalyptus in California. According to the company's 1911 prospectus, "The forests concerned in these pages were planted with a clear understanding of the situation. The company now sees plainly that it possesses a source of emolument [profit] higher than the average gold mine — the idea so long associated with California wealth ... No teak, mahogany, ebony, hickory, or oak was ever tougher, denser, stronger or of more glorious hardness than this swift growing Eucalyptus of California .... A ten years supply would be the total from which the huge building operations of the world could draw were there no other trees planted."

ALBANY HILL

The tall cross[14] at the top of the hill was not planted to memorialize the dead.[15] It rises cool as a new cigarette. Were it a crucifix: An electrical outlet for Jesus's pained mouth. There are a couple of benches facing it, toothless pews. A couple of chapped lips.

It was not that we were further up, but perhaps the act of ascending

> maybe eucalyptus
> filled our eyes and
> gagged the traffic
> which makes me bleary.

[14] The cross is white, 20 – 25 feet tall, and bears a Lion's Club insignia. Around Christmas and Easter, it is lit up and glows white atop the hill.

[15] In 1905, 23 employees of the Judson Powder Works were killed in a massive accidental nitroglycerine explosion. After this accident, dynamite production was moved to less-densely settled areas to the north. The explosion also hewed a huge crater in the north flank of Albany Hill, visible today as a dip in the tree line. The cross was placed on the hill to commemorate a member of the local Lion's Club who owned a large swath of land on Albany Hill.

The single-story suburban tract houses and the eucalyptus here minded me of home, Torrance. Could have been the street I grew up on, but for the hills, asphalt waves rolling. My town was flat, except for the hill behind my house.

There were many eucalyptus trees in my backyard, until some got sick and had to be chopped down. I was mad that my parents hired men to chop them at all, slice with big electrical saws like industrial platypuses, but jounced on their felled branches anyway with my mother, brother, and sister. Now there are three trees, bending over slightly with arms in yoga repose, dangling tire swings for years. Three mothers, or perhaps firm echoes of my sister, brother, and me.

In the summer, the hill is covered in dry, matted grass and wild radish gone to seed. But at this time of year, after days of rain like we've had up here in the East Bay, the hill is purple and white with buds of wild radishes long enough to serve as swords when pulled up. I always called mine Sting.[16]

We four say the Bay in sharp, post-rain high definition from some street in Richmond.

A few nights before, I had a dream: My father and me, walking in my hometown. We were walking up a hill. Going to visit my old elementary, talking about – what, I forget, never good at remembering words to begin with and they less memorizeable in dreams.[17] It was the golden hour. Although definitely Hometown, it was Berkeley in the dream – not Torrance. As we crested the hill, my father and I saw

> The San Francisco
> Bay spread out before us,
> unfolded blue accordion.

The sun was just beginning to set, suspended for a moment over the horizon like it was holding its breath, deciding whether to dive. A whole flock of white sea birds flew from the sun or the horizon or the Golden Gate bridge toward us. As they passed above, we could see their wings were tinged gold from the setting sun.

I told my mother about the dream in a phone call and she said, *kheir inshallah*[18]: maybe it was portent of me coming home, and asked, Do you always dream in color?

I asked Anna if she dreamt in color. Anna said yes, she did dream in color, but her dreams were soundless. I thought maybe we dream in color because of the TV we grew up with. The music in my dreams makes my insides flip.

[16] Named after Bilbo's sword in Tolkein's *The Hobbit* and *The Lord of the Rings*. Sting was cast by the elves to serve as a knife, but Bilbo could use it as a sword due to his small hobbit stature. He named the sword after using it to fight off massive spiders in Mirkwood forest and later bequeathed it to Frodo. Sting glowed blue when orcs were near.

[17] Had a dream in which I was taking ASL lessons. Not American Sign Language, but Architectural Sign Language. Buildings spoke different dialects depending on their construction materials. Brick and cinder-block constructions understood movements of a different shape than steel-and-glass structures; their grammars differed from those made of wood. In my studies I had attained a remarkable fluency … additions, renovations, demolitions of their structures; they told me histories of the land on which they were built, and the people who had lived within them. When I awoke, this entire language had disappeared.

[18] Arabic. Literally, "good blessings/if it's God's will." A listener will say this before being told a dream. Most generally, the phrase expresses hope for the future.

5201 VAN FLEET AVENUE
Richmond, CA

On Van Fleet just past the Eastshore Freeway. What a pleasant street, and so light on the tongue. Houses so sweet, and the flowers, too.

We walked down to the street's end in a cul de sac because we saw something written on the tan shingles of a house's sharply-sloping roof:

> "This street
> Floods!!!
> ask why
> 510-620-6512
> x1
> cityofprideandpurpose.com"[19]

I later searched Google Maps for a second look at the house. In its images, there is no chalk or paint on the roof, and a man sitting (or perhaps leaning) on the front porch is blurred out beyond visibility.

> photo evidences dry
> season with patches
> of yellowing grass.

No sooner had they dried out than the heavens brought more rain, and the water started rising to their doorstep once again.[20]

In the lapping water, objects floated.
Trash. Oily substances. A syringe.[21]

Years ago, I, prophetic, dreamt my front yard flooded. It reached up
a bit past the ankles, but remained clear. When it flooded in real life,
I asked my mama, how high's the water?[22] She said, just below your
ankles.

[19] "City of Pride and Purpose" is the Richmond city motto. Although Richmond has a longstanding history of hosting heavy industry, it has been recasting its economy on the basis of service and retail since the 1970s.

[20] Language adapted from a song by Jason Myers, resident (with his wife, Maria) of the house with the painted roof. The couple purchased the house in 2003, and soon found that it and they fell victim to regular flooding due to improper street drainage. It is not the city of Richmond, but a private French company — Veolia Environnement SA — that is responsible for the area's wastewater and storm-drain systems.

[21] Language borrowed from a speech given by Maria Myers at a Richmond city council meeting.

[22] See Johnny Cash's tune, "Five Feet High and Rising."

We crossed the highway and walked West, away from hunched
Costco, toward the water. Path bordered by sourgrass and wild fennel
we picked till our tongues tingled. Wild radish's purple and white
petals. I picked a bundle of mugwort and put it in my inner pocket.
I knew mugwort as one of the nine Saxon magic herbs. What magic,
I didn't know. Pon said if I put it under my pillow I'd have vivid
dreams, or erotic. Patrick said he'd smoke what he took.

Along the water, only egrets and an old woman, walking home. Asked
after her accent: she replied yes, she was German. From Munich.

Shelf mushrooms turned into plates, place-holders for rocks on the
shore. Climbing a discarded segment of concrete stairs, I looked to be
in an Escher painting sprinkled on some windswept shore, rain-torn
post storm. It was cool, the silver light. Like everything had already
been preserved in tintype. A kind of photograph.

Anna took pictures of:

> My post-industrial-sludge-covered boots,
> gooey green.[25]

> Our friend the dead sting ray. Even without arms,
> he looked like Jesus. Disc width of fins spread.
> Mouth a slit, gap. Sting ray who died for our sins.

Pon's new quarter next to him for scientific reference.

Mussel shells.

Live mussels.

Barnacles living on porcelain plates.

Barnacles living on porcelain mugs.

Pon, triumphant, with a fistful of mug handles.

My finger beside hermit crab who had adopted two plate pieces for his home.

An old TEPCO flyer:

> "Good china
> makers are not to be found
> in the labor-market —
> they must be made."[26]

Our wide-angle view: the Bay Bridge and the Golden Gate. And a grey gauzy veil of cloud, specter disintegrating over San Francisco.

[23] Technical Porcelain and Chinaware Company. Major producer of plates and other porcelain kitchen wares for hotels and restaurants across the West Coast. The company, founded by Italian immigrant John Pagliero, also received contracts with the Navy, Army, and Veterans Administration. Based in El Cerrito from the 1930s until its closure in 1968, TEPCO was El Cerrito's largest employer for many of those years. As of 2010, El Cerrito's top employers were the West Contra Costa Unified School District and Home Depot.

[24] The beach's local name. It is located on the south shore of Point Isabel. When TEPCO was shut down, it was granted a selective permit from the sanitation department to dump mal-manufactured wares there, as well as its surplus china remaining at that time.

[25] On November 7, 2007, more than 200,000 liters of oil spilled into the San Francisco Bay after the *Cosco Busan*, a container ship, struck a tower of the SF-Oakland Bay Bridge, which was obscured by a thick fog. Many beaches in the San Francisco and East Bays were temporarily closed, including Point Isabel.

[26] Despite this flyer promoting company investment in employees and compassionate corporatism, TEPCO suffered from labor issues. In the late 1930s, factory employees went on strike and there was a fire at the factory. After WWII, there was an explosion at the factory.

Alone in the afternoon I biked back to TEPCO Beach. Under the
overpass where a man lived with a pile of cans
        (could he be any man,
        in any city?)
across the street from the COSTCO
        (through the bushes,
        over a little dirt,
        past a Chinese man fishing,
        clear line deep in muggy water).

The truth is pretty easy to arrange, isn't it?
I didn't see anything – I'd like
        (I, I, I – it's enough to make your stomach turn)
time to be re arranged.

Asked, where's TEPCO? But no one knew.
Asked a man crossing the street, hey, do you know – where's TEPCO
Beach?

Even worse than someone looking at you crazy is looking past, you
don't exist.
If I'm not, then
I must really be out of my mind.

Maybe I'd never been there because I had never been there –

Explanations more reasonable than high murky tide:

Maybe I'd followed, fallen – through the labyrinth, down the hole, into a hurricane (been carried by), through a portal, a porthole between worlds – that closes up behind you once passed-through: as imaginary, into the imaginary[27] after all, cardinal rule broken: never show it to anyone else, they won't believe you. Sharing magic with impure intention, like using flight to woo a date.[28]

[27] *Pan's Labyrinth*: through the gnarl'd trees. *Wizard of Oz*. David Bowie's *Labyrinth*. *Alice in Wonderland*. ET's hiding place. The door marked by moonlight hitting it just right. Platform 9 ¾.

[28] Intention, or *niyya* in Arabic, is a central tenet of Islam, stemming from a concept of "doing what is beautiful," in which motivation rather than the act itself fulfills the definition of beauty.

TEPCO BEACH
2015

A few years passed before I showed it to anyone else.

We woke in the dark, before work, to discover magic at a special hour.

By bus across from COSTCO (the hour too early for BART)

between the bushes, over a little dirt, past dirty water, shallower now
at early hour –

TEPCO as sun rose
melting mist, lit
me and Ariana, in the glim.

I wrote a love story in my head. Story of love for a new body, like an
alien inhabiting itself, the self a new planet. The body has changed.
Once, twice, girth, height, a few-lifetimes-for-one deal.

> We took home pieces of the beach.
> Mine I'm sure I later lost
> despite keeping it close pocketed
> token of home, for a little while.

Ultralight beam[29] driving up as the sun broke through the clouds: sang its aubade:[30]

> a goodbye, oh god –
> sun burned our eyes,
> sand, shells, and
> stone: a double awareness.

We sat and stared out on a log of concrete, so pocked with rocks it couldn't be called 'stone' or made more romantic.

Love wasn't there.
May as well have been alone.
This place in my language: a kanji symbol
to tell someone you're special,
dear to me. Meaning instilled
by visits spanning a season.
A season drawn out
into years, coated
in alternate weathers.

Connecting to others turned me inward, ultimately

an appreciation of beauty's just not enough.

This is weird,[31]
but I've read about so much
weirder in books,[32]
he didn't actually say, but I imagined he felt.

[29] Upon a second listening, *Life of Pablo* is "not my favorite" Kanye album.

[30] "Dawn song," a poetic form. Often expressing lovers' regret of parting at daybreak. Some scholars trace the form's origins to the cries of medieval watchmen announcing the night's passing and returning day from their towers. My mind turns to Islam's pre-dawn call to prayer; I discover a surprising note of resonance with Europe. In The Spirit of Romance (1910), Ezra Pound marked the dawn of romance literature with a Provencal "Alba" from around the 10th century:

> Dawn appeareth upon the sea, from behind the hill, The watch / Passeth, it shineth clear amid the shadows.

[31] Dali could've thunk it up.

[32] *Gravity's Rainbow*, for instance.

First heard of the Bulb from Asa Dodsworth,[34] whom I ran into one February or March. He was collecting curbed Christmas firs in a quilted textile fanny pack, looked like something from Lhasa Karnak. Told me about the annual burn at the Bulb. Never did see it, but saw the pit when I ended up at the Bulb years later, imagined sparks flying.

First visit, Jimbow the Librarian read from a book, page's edges burned.[35] Not prophecies, but truths. "And here it says September, and their ages are nine and eleven years old, so we're thinking about 9/11 – " and this word means that, frighteningly accurate, this cultural consciousness. Not tortoise shell or ox scapulae. No plastron cracks. No yarrow, just books for an Albany oracle. The burning more integral than the body burned.

[33] A man-made bulbous promontory jutting into the San Francisco Bay. In 1939, the Santa Fe Railroad dynamited a small hill southwest of Albany Hill to build the Golden Gate Fields racetracks, adjacent to the Albany Bulb. Remaining debris was pushed into the Bay. In 1963, the Santa Fe Railroad signed a contract with the City of Albany, and the area officially became a landfill for construction debris. Between 1963 and 1983, about two million cubic yards of building debris were dumped into the Bay, creating the 60-acre chunk of land known as the Bulb today. Due to the efforts of Save the Bay, dumping trash was forbidden in the 1980s and people began to reside on the land and made it their home, constructing shelters and creating large-scale art installations.

[34] A Berkeley Rent Stabilization Commissioner.

[35] Early on the morning of January 12, 2014 the library, which was built by Jimbow and fellow Bulb resident Andy Kreamer in 2006, was burned to the ground. The cause of the fire was unknown. Prior to its destruction, the library contained 300-400 books.

Kouros came last-minute because he was Sad, not Political.[36] Drive-by: bring a sleeping bag – spontaneous most delicious when rare, sure to stale later.

Joined Baylor, Nancy, Lindsay, me. Nancy slept in the car with a guitar. Cold cold night. Rest slept girl-boy-girl-boy on a flat concrete slab, up-jut. After singing all the songs we knew late into the night, some silence, in chorus felt like more than four.

Temporary Autonomous Zone,[37] did we leave a mark? Presence residue in the Air? Cryogenic protest ova?

Enclosure, night-egg, burrowed against cold, with one friend's hand in each of mine, we were hands on a clock that spins, nix ticks; second, minute, hour arranged by height, not time.

Baylor played *I Love You Dad* and *Jim Wise*[38] from his phone
early a.m., strange peace waking
to songs
so sad
I looked and looked at Kouros's eyes. For the first time. They hovered between colors.

What if every person who's a person to you were an actor? (I say to myself from within my own head.) Not like *Truman Show*, more like

Joseph Campbell. Every one a dream symbol: loose tooth, king, dog.
Or more – each person a planet revolving laden with meaning? As a
God?

> My life's ruled
> by a rotation
> of living Gods.
> Sometimes they transfer
> bodies, as in a dream.

[36] In 2013, the City of Albany proposed developing the Bulb into formal parkland, and began removing residents. In March 2014, four friends and I headed to camp out on the Bulb in protest, yet found no one else there that night. Our efforts, along with those of many others and the admirable efforts of Bulb residents who spoke out at city council meetings and created documentaries publicly available on YouTube telling their stories and those of their homes, did not have the desired impact. In 2014, Bulb residents were offered $3000 each to leave their homes. Ownership of the Albany Bulb has since been transferred to the State Parks. As of 2017, the Bulb is still in an uninhabited limbo.

[37] "The TAZ is like an uprising which does not engage directly with the State, a guerilla operation which liberates an area (of land, of time, of imagination) and then dissolves itself to re-form elsewhere / elsewhen, *before* the State can crush it."
— Hakim Bey

[38] Sun Kil Moon's album *Benji* had come out that year and we were obsessed with it.

TO TONY'S HOUSE

From just south of Alca-Tel in Oakland, North to
———— Avenue, border of Berkeley and Albany, slightly to the West
(into the sea?). A four mile walk I took twice a week, usually with
a break about two miles in on Shattuck, a cup of coffee, a talk with
somebody or with luck, work at my other job, before continuing
down as Shattuck becomes Henry just past the Safeway, Henry into
Sutter, through the Northbrae Tunnel[39] (as opposed to up the stairs
and over, leading to – Los Angeles Avenue, Indian Rock, Marin Circle
Fountain) spit out onto Solano, past the Wells Fargo, sometimes
absentmindedly up Colusa but usually continuing and walking with
the elementary school fence, brambles poking out of it, to my right,
past the house as I curved to the left where a woman played piano
at exactly two o'clock daily, green pilot light behind the white lacy
curtains out of which the music drifted, a garden being drought-
replanted below a wooden fence, and then the knuckle-bump of
a street that was its own world, the entrance to it overgrown very
green, big-leaved, lemon tree, little Honda blessed by Meher Baba,
spreading tree in front with ivy grown around it, ivy around a big
palm too, two trees whose roots crack up the red stone walk and steps
to Tony's porch, to Tony's house, the screen door before the wooden
door cracked open to let me in, or call me the breeze,[40] the plum tree's
leaves, the buzzing doorbell I never pressed on purpose.

[39] Originally built for the Southern Pacific Railroad in 1910, as a commuter electric railroad tunnel. Closed when train service ended in 1958. Became a city street in 1963.

[40] J.J. Cale.

First tea, a talk, then work – as if the two were separate. A break for lunch, we talk again. Kasha sometimes at first, then the famous sandwich: Ezekiel bread bought in bulk, frozen then thawed, Laura Scudder peanut butter, sharp cheddar cheese (all generous portions of course). Salt, bread-and-butter pickle, jalapeño from a jar, Arugula or whatever other greens were handy, green onion perhaps? On a rare special occasion: matzo with homemade guacamole. Never thought, how to pay the bills. A week's work stretched into six months at least. Always before leaving, tea and a cool mint chocolate Clif Bar[41] cut perfectly in half with a knife, never broken. Is it unnecessary to say – a man of precision.

[41] "Born on a 175-mile bike ride," the company is based in Emeryville, CA. This regular Clif Bar consumption with a loved one was my first experience in customer loyalty, being grandfathered into a product through positive association.

Riverside/Moreno County

Mountains on one side (the northerly) – buildings, rock-colored, on the
other. The living, operating rubble of our existence. The mountains,
they are watching, littered with eyes. We are actually the afterthings.
All these identical, terra-cotta rooftops, unnaturally arranged.
Sculpted land with boxes placed on it. Labeled boxes. Storing people,
a network of preservation, rows and rows, channels and channels,
ravines and ravines, columns and columns. Signifying relation, loci
passive-aggressively explain orders, "just to give you an idea …" this is
where the salt and vinegar will pass.

> scree, ravines, cold
> desert bright
> like china

Sneaker-destruction videos are a YouTube genre I haven't dipped into
yet – never will, realistically – but the possibility exists to be tapped,
extracted to fuel our future.

> Beaumont.
> Banning.
> Inning.

name's edge familiar

Furrows filled with light and, you know, other words you haven't had reason to think of in some time but which are pleasing to speak.

Crystal mountains, craggy chandeliers.
Who knew mountains don't root to the earth, but hang from the sky?
Who knew?

Cloud shadows blue, dark blue, transferring night sky onto the ground, strange deal day has with clouds, plays pretend it's another time in certain zones, zones that drift. Drifting zones of night and day that cool the ground, allow moisture its time there, sweeten the earth before releasing it. Periods of fogging followed by lifting (yes, that is revealing).

By-along the San Bernardino Mountains, down the 10 Freeway I think (could Google-Maps it right now, but won't) Tony sends me a painting. I see it on my phone, palm-sized blessing, totem, amulet. Hold the image of his painting up against the cliffs –

> it's cliff-shade, somewhere
> between yellow and trying
> to make life a poem.

A boy is stuck up and must be right all the time. It's exhausting.

I have found a special affinity with geological shades' rhyme with those I love. So Tony was in the vicinity, the tangible as well as electro-telepathic realm.

Sometimes I feel like a square of color, just being placed against things.

I ask for – contrast? Some species of intention, at least.

A semi-permanent autonomous zone and off-the-grid community in the California Badlands.

Near the Salton Sea,[44] which roils brown, smells like death, sweats dead fish out onto the shore where they lay in various stages of decay – some have eyes, others hollows, layers of fish bones, shards of gill and fin sun-bleached and delicate, spall upon touch.

Salvation Mountain's trees and peaks made of two-by-fours and hay covered with plaster and paint smack in the middle of desert flats. Salvation Mountain says, Jesus Comes Inside You. Young people's skepticism of religion confuses me. Guess I'm not around it much. Salvation Mountain, a curiously soft landscape in the aridity of that region, where the hard earth is cracked into scales you can lift individually like plates. I like this construction, which tricks you into believing that you might be living in the earth.

[43] The work of Leonard Knight.

[44] Not a proper sea, but a salty, man-made lake I remember first seeing on a map of California at the age of nine.

Daytrip from LA, who knew
these worlds were so near
one another

Woke to gunshots, not for the first time on this trip.[45] The extra-terrestrial regions of America, good for target practice. But there are pet puppies too, sandy domesticity. Only learned one man's story – and with permission took his photograph, with the camera Nalini lent me. Mostly landscapes till then, and Spencer's fingers touching paws with nails painted pink. He'd moved here with his wife: she had brain cancer, they had no insurance. What's one, what are two, to do?

Harvest energy
from dumpster batteries:
prepare for post-human.

POINT ISABEL PARK

We walked and walked over pretty grass – gentle mounds of soft tufts, what I called "Chinese grass" as a kid. An angry neighbor bordered his plot with bright orange string to keep kids from splaying on it.

Memorial benches scattered throughout the park provided stunning Bay views, carry messages about loving dogs, and ocean metaphors: ebbs, flows, time, tides, horizons, waves – One plaque claimed eternal life: Sean 1952 – onward. 1952, also the year of my mother's birth. Guilty amusement at the claim to infinity.

POINT ISABEL PARK

We heard the woman and her son before we saw them.

More the woman. She held a saxophone, shiny and new; her son, a
blue plastic trombone. They drove to the ocean to play together on the
shore. Mother gold with her little boy blue, come to blow their horns.

Boy's arm retreating
and flowing as shoreline
moving trombone's slide.

A trombone's spit valve is also called the water key.

Mama shimmied like
Lisa Simpson, all yellow
as she played, swaying

> My mother listens to a saxophonist who plays on the outer
> edge of the parking lot for the pier near which we live. He
> plays facing a boulder-bordered beach, notes echoing in the
> open space of the parking structure before exiting as an orb,
> some sort of spirit. When she tells me about his songs on
> the phone, my mother pronounces "saxophone" like
> "sex-o-phone."

I walked backwards: heels slow, eyes closed. Pretended my ears were shaped like trumpet mouths better to catch the sound.

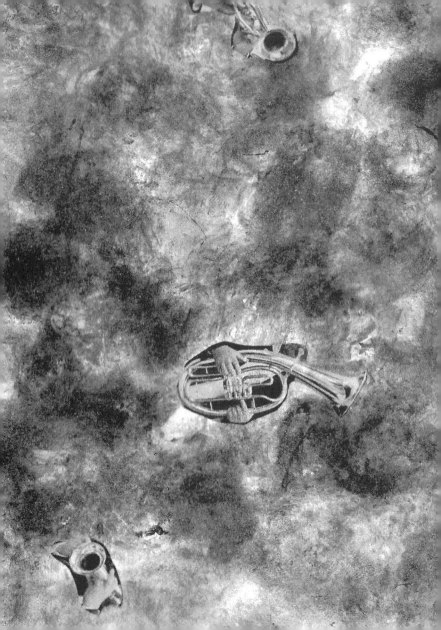

UNITED STATES POSTAL SERVICE SORT FACILITY
Richmond, CA[46]

Chain-link fences kept us from the rows of empty postal trucks. Too
bad: I wanted to burrow in one and be delivered. Their back doors all
open, like so many mouths hung slack, quacking.

I imagined this was a place
where dreams are manufactured,
readied for delivery.

[46] Sort facilities are where postal workers and machines sort mail so that it can ultimately reach its final destination. According to numerous reports, packages often get lost, mysteriously disappear, or are "held hostage" at the USPS Sort Facility in Richmond.

Books no one wants. Dick and Jane, Spot. Hot hot hot. Cold off the presses. Westerns. Ian was very excited to find a copy of a hacking zine from maybe 1993 tucked away between them all. *I wonder what hacking even was then*, he geeked out. I wonder what kind of computer my brother had then. Not yet the Quantex I later inherited, kicked softly with socked toes.

1990s hacking in my born-in-1992 memory is:

Singing tones to payphones, imitating quarters.[47]

Brother and sister called home collect from movie theater payphones when they were done, so mom and dad knew to pick them up. I never was allowed to go alone and couldn't try it. Once tried calling a friend from a payphone at a desolate beach to cry in someone's ear, but either I couldn't remember the number right, or the phone was out of service. Slapped it right back into its cradle.

Remember: hacking is more than just a crime: it's a survival trick.[48]

Mama taught me a trick to avoid paying postage: write your intended recipient's address on the RETURN portion of the envelope, and drop it in a mailbox. Tried this once, but it wasn't the 1990s anymore.

[47] While this trick may have been used in the 1990s, it is actually a vestige of the 1970s, when hacker Captain Crunch (real name, John Draper) made long-distance phone calls for free by blowing a whistle that he found in a Captain Crunch cereal box into a payphone. Later, a magazine called the "Youth International Party Line / Technical Assistance Program" or YIPL / TAP was founded to help phreaks (long-distance phone hackers) make long-distance phone calls for no charge.

[48] A line from *Hackers* (1995), starring a very young and pretty Angelina Jolie, and Jonny Lee Miller. It's basically a film about hackers saving the world. My brother and I watched it together when I was about 11, and he took care to tell me that hacking doesn't actually looks like the film's psyched-out depictions, although it does bring joy.

Amidst the jumble, Pon found two copies of *The Hobbit*, side by side. One became mine. I read it on the BART ride home instead of speaking. My copy was from the library of a certain Mr. Stout, who by a sticker on the inside cover reminded me that it still belongs to him with an imperative *RETURN it*! after enjoying.

I had read *The Hobbit* the summer before entering the fourth grade because my brother forced me to. I identified with the short but brave protagonist, and started in on *The Lord of the Rings* immediately after. I talked my parents into buying me a copy with all three volumes bound in a flimsy soft cover from a big bookstore on Santa Monica's Third Street.[49] Costing more than twenty dollars, the book seemed expensive, and I felt a pang of unnecessary guilt. Swallowing this, I petted its glossy front.[50]

One of the first few days of the fourth grade was September 11, 2001. Mama touched my elbow before I clambered from her car that morning. *Don't tell anyone you're Iraqi, okay?* I didn't understand why anyone would ask where I was from. What am I supposed to say? *Tell them you're Lebanese.* Nodded empty assent.

that day, green knit jacket,
tag "MADE IN IRAQ"
scratched at my neck.

I soon began having nightmares so intense I could no longer keep *The Lord of the Rings* in my room. Snuck it onto my brother's bookshelf.

People I knew would pull off their familiar casings, abandoning them to jiggle like the flimsy rubber masks in B-grade horror movies, or synthetic breasts devoid of their scarred chests.[51]

They revealed themselves dark,
hooded figures with charred bodies;
peered through the big bay
windows of my living room
as I cowered beneath the couch.

In dreams, I ran away from other kids
in school hallways and on the playground.
My house when I returned home was emptied of adults.

[49] "Santa Monica's world-famous alfresco Third Street Promenade dining and shopping experience includes casual and fine dining restaurants, on a bustling pedestrian-only landscape."

[50] The cover bore images from the feature film adaptations of the books, the first of which had been released that year.

[51] In *The Fellowship of the Ring*, the hobbits are instructed to be wary even of those whom they recognize, as dark riders can disguise themselves as familiar flesh.

At twelve years old, I finally finished reading *The Lord of the Rings*. In Beirut: there, architecture is battles layered, power stories.

A city rebuilding
itself yellowing stone
and oppressive air.[52]

In my memory, Beirut exists as small pictures:

Gaping buildings, mouths howling Munchian, laundry lines strung like dental floss through teeth: collared shirts, children's dresses, all hanging still in balm-heavy air.

Corinthian columns I could touch. The color of old paper, ornate, rising from a smog-sooted intersection.

A spray of bullet holes on a shady wall. I did not finger the grooves of cool concrete, despite the city's heat.

Soldiers in army fatigues, leaning on arm-length black rifles like green figurines, guarding the McDonald's.[53]

The constant toots of car horns for weddings: I want mine to be like this – a caravan of noise. Only thing for which I want an automobile: an unraveling-me parade.[54]

[52] Planning and zoning are virtually nonexistent in Beirut, which, although an over urbanized city center today, still adheres to the organic structure of an Islamic city in many ways: densely gathered streets, many of which loop into closed cul-de-sacs. Islamic cities are sometimes said to be characterized by their "formlessness and irregular mass of confusion." Despite the existence of a large Christian population – it's common to see pork items on restaurant menus – Beirut is structurally, very much an "Islamic" city. Before the Civil War began in 1975 (it lasted for 15 years), Beirut was considered the most completely Westernized city in the Middle East. The war destroyed many newer developments. However, by the time I visited in 2004, Beirut was in the process of being rebuilt, and to my eyes, had been much revived. This was the work of join-stock company *Solidière*, which was commissioned to implement a plan for and re-build central Beirut, eighty percent of which had been destroyed during the war. *Solidière* was controlled in large part by Lebanon's then-Prime Minister (and multi-billionaire) Rafiq Hariri. Hariri was assassinated in 2005. *Solidière* continues.

[53] My sister explained to me that there had been attempts to blow the McDonald's up, as many Lebanese viewed it as a corporate outpost of American imperialism. The year I visited Lebanon, there had been at least four bombing attempts on American fast food outlets in Beirut. Since the beginning of the Iraq occupation in 2003, American businesses and Western embassies in Lebanon had been provided with armed guards by internal security forces.

[54] In Lebanon, as in much of the Arab world, it is traditional for wedding attendants to follow behind the newlyweds in their cars, honking their horns. A frequent feature of Beirut's aural landscape.

EL CERRITO CHINESE CHRISTIAN CHURCH
6830 Stockton Ave, El Cerrito, CA 94530

Black saints with rice paper faces look at God. Cigarette filters for
some sun. I'm lucky to be passing by when there's still light on this
grey day, stony-faced sky.

A more tenderly stained
glass, tinder. And any
color will do.

I look and look and wait and wait. But there are no people inside –
only leaflets and leaflets and an after-hours thrill.

EL CERRITO HIGH SCHOOL[55]
540 Ashbury Avenue, El Cerrito, CA 94530

Path to the high school is bleary, or maybe only I am, walking
sleepy like a dirty blanket dragged behind a drunk. Football field's
immaculate green – such a vision! Makes me want to iron my clothes
and streak *naked across the lawn*.

Blackberry brambles,
Lemon trees
Along the way, but –

Empty lot by the parking
lot holds ghosts of old gardens,
now all wood platforms, raised
beds raising nothing.

[55] The high school was originally built as a Works Progress Administration project in the late 1930s, and has since been reconstructed. It is an example of Brutalist architecture, an aggressive style popular from the 1950s to the 1970s. Brutalist architecture is characterized by large, highly linear and box-like forms of poured concrete with little embellishment or other decoration. It is a low-cost form popular for schools and shopping centers as well as low-income housing projects and prisons.

SEAVIEW DRIVE
El Cerrito, CA

West side of the cemetery,
Western border,
Road an ocean
The dead fear falling
into – houses, cliffs.

The ocean isn't visible from Seaview Drive – just houses, suburban,
some with their gray entrails splayed on front lawns, tubes expelled
like afterbirth, but cleanly, or maybe they'd been neutered, boilers,
radiators, and other heat pulled out.

Some have gates in their back yards that open into the cemetery[56] –
where ghosts can pass between their conjoined worlds, tend to their
own lawns while the gravekeepers ride over their bodies.[57]

[56] I know because I asked a guy (grey shirt, balding) where I could find an entrance to the cemetery, and he told me about these gates. He did not have such a gate in his backyard, and could not tell me why they existed in the first place.

[57] San Franciscans, worried about ghouls who "held vandalish orgies … on moonless, foggy nights" and ransacked graves, relocated their dead (San Francisco News, June 20, 1939). Burials and cremations are no longer permitted in the city. In the East Bay, there are many cemeteries and the living evidently reside more comfortably beside their dead.

SUNSET VIEW CEMETERY[58]
December 1, 2012

The true entrance too far a passage, ended up hopping a flimsy barbed-wire fence to enter.[59]

The ocean isn't visible until you're in the cemetery. There, it's a million-dollar view for the dead, carefully pruned.

What has a good ring to it doesn't make it true.

My mother told me she recently stood in front of the ocean yelling, *What is this?!* As if she'd genuinely forgotten, or as though it were a foreign thing quite outside the imagination, or as if she'd just arrived there from the grave.

There are stones, urns, and mausoleums here. A container for every form. There are water and willows and bonsai trees. There was a man in long spandex on a bicycle, who stopped by a grave and stood.

You can trace the demographics in the deaths,

> names, faces, flowers
> on the graves, the city's
> sea-change[60] over time.

I'd like to map this city within, below, at the outskirts of the city, project it over the original – it would be far bigger, would gently burst at the borders, cast itself like clouds shading the streets and interstates and hills and faults of El Cerrito.[61]

I'd like to wed a dead man, maybe, compliment him on his fine digs,[62] wrap his moustache round my neck and wear it like a collar of starched marble, hold it in my hand and whip through the cemetery knocking softly at graves.[63]

[58] The cemetery was established in 1908, prior to El Cerrito's incorporation as a city in 1917. Before this time, it mainly served the Berkeley population.

[59] Entering this way initially placed me, I think, somewhere in the center of the cemetery.

[60] In *The Tempest* (possibly Shakespeare's last play), the spirit Ariel sings a song to comfort Ferdinand after his father has drowned to death:

> Full fathom five thy father lies,
> Of his bones are coral made,
> Those are pearls that were his eyes,
> Nothing of him doth fade,
> But doth suffer a sea-change,
> into something rich and strange,
> Sea-nymphs hourly ring his knell,
> Ding-dong.
> Hark! now I hear them, ding-dong, bell.

[61] Walking through the cemetery, I noticed an interesting temporal transformation. Older graves almost exclusively bore European names, while recent graves were more diverse – they feature many names carved in Mandarin, and photographs of the dead and their families reveal that there are many more Black and Hispanic residents today than there were at the turn of the 20th century. Indeed, the cemetery provides an easy and interesting representation of demographic change in El Cerrito over time. In 1950 (the earliest year for which El Cerrito census data on race was available at the time of this writing), the population was 92.3 percent white (about seven percent of this population was comprised of new European immigrants, while the remainder were "Native" whites). Not until the 2000s did the white population drop into the fifty-percent range (to 57.8%, from 65.6% in 1990, 72.5% in 1980, 86.3% in 1970). According

to data from the 2010 census, the city's population was 53.3% white, 27.3% Asian, 11.1% Hispanic/Latino, 7.7% black and 6.5% mixed race. Indigenous people represented less than one percent of the population. Chinese residents represent the biggest portion of El Cerrito's Asian population.

[62] Term thrown about in the 1990s to refer to a place of residence.

[63] I was struck by the image of one J. Tambacopoulos on his gravestone. His birth-year in the 1800s was unknown and he died in 1921, yet there was a very stately and not-much worn photograph of him on the gravestone, featuring a very fine moustache.

SUNSET VIEW CEMETERY
September 7, 2013

Jefferson and I lounge and roll down the yard, snap a disposable
camera, photographs I did not develop for months afterwards. I
can pretend that I am purposeful, busy rather than lazy, stretch this
productive lounging like a canvas or a screen and give the good ghosts
within it time to emerge and be caught unwary. He took a picture of
me beside a girl's grave because I thought I looked like her. Now I'm
not so sure, guess I won't be unless I look again.

NEW HAVEN, CONNECTICUT

The Green[64] white after storm, like a beach. And we maybe whales.
We grew numb from the feet up[65] without noticing, I mean, who
would really – hot on top and inside really. Sachin made pterodactyl
noises for his hot joy, ponytail a torpedo. And I guess I laughed for
mine, mostly to be with them all – Sudani refugees and math PhDs
– none of us natives. And also joy of looking for nothing beyond
reality:[66] scoring goals, pounding feet, pointing toes, falling into wet
sweater sticking to elbows,[67]

> start of March, last snow – morning
> plan: slide like legg'd fish on
> sun, half past four

Maybe they've got dragon breath too, misting up under my heels,
slipping me. Ghosts needn't spite by definition – although I might,
if buried in corset and crinoline wide as goal posts. Maybe they're
chittering quiet underfoot, melting snow, our yips and ha-s! tickling
them, six feet below or has the earth eroded?

Maybe we're all of us the same age, and they're playing too.

After, before Richter's,[68] Brian and Sachin took me for ice cream. In
Spring, Bogdan would ask me to the bar not out of ulterior design,
but because he is Romanian.[69] For now it's good to keep sixteen, with
friends old enough who want just to play soccer, buy me a scoop.

[64] The New Haven Green is a 16-acre park located in the center of New Haven, Connecticut's downtown area. The Green was the main burial ground for New Haven residents until 1821, when most of the bodies were relocated to Grove Street Cemetery. However, it's estimated that five to ten thousand bodies remain buried beneath the Green.

[65] From Edgar Lee Masters' *Minerva Jones*:
> And I sank into death, growing numb from the feet up / Like one stepping deeper and deeper into a stream of ice

[66] From Wallace Stevens' *An Ordinary Evening in New Haven*:
> We seek / Nothing beyond reality

[67] When I asked my Uncle Jed to join in snow soccer, he responded: "Really, your parents should get you special accident insurance given your proclivity for self-injury and lack of general awareness of basic safety."

[68] Now closed, once a pub on Chapel Street. Sold beer by the yard, known also to sell super snow soccer energy drinks in giant carafes.

[69] There is no legal drinking age in Romania.

CHAPEL OF THE CHIMES[70]
Summer Solstice,[71] 2015

A series of trances we enter together.

A man with a guitar and a woman with a sitar, a dialogue in two languages. Responding, sifting, moving beyond language.

Eli who'd played Woody, fiddling with a troupe.

Our voices (whose?) melding with those of many strangers, in melodies invented on the spot.

My favorite musical moments are those I can't hold: once

> siphoned into my
> ears, like hourglasses, in which
> sound's transformed into
> liquid time.

Cornered Beth Custer[72] in search of Oleg Karavaychuk's[73] 1976 score to *Chemi Bebia*,[74] but she was in the process of moving and had lost track of her possessions.

Can't for the life of me remember whom I was with that day, but do remember the feel of open space indoors, light negotiated by windows, arches, fountains, and photosynthetic shading; niches with vessels parenthetical, pear-shaped like hip-to-waist ratios, book-shaped urns, words or spirits of words preserved after ash.

[70] A crematorium and columbarium. Originally founded in 1909, it was expanded in 1928 due to population growth and the increasing popularity of cremation. The 1928 renovations were based on the designs of Julia Morgan, California's first licensed woman architect. She is buried in the adjacent Mountain View Cemetery. A later renovation was made in 1959 by Frank Lloyd Wright's protégé Aaron Green. John Lee Hooker's ashes are located in Chapel of the Chimes.

[71] On every summer solstice since 1996, an event called "Garden of Memory," in which over 40 musicians play avant garde and experiemntal music, has been held at the Chapel of the Chimes. The event was conceived of by journalist Sarah Cahill while she was researching an article about interesting local public bathrooms for the *East Bay Express*. Hearing organ music as she wandered through the maze-like columbarium, Cahill was intrigued by the way sound functioned in the space. An accomplished pianist in her own right, she pitched the idea for a concert there to board members of New Music Bay Area, and has organized the event ever since.

[72] A San Francisco-based clarinetist and composer.

[73] A composer born in 1927, in Soviet Ukraine. He composed scores for at least 66 films, and died in 2016. That same year a documentary about him entitled *Oleg and the Strange Arts* by Venezuelan director Andrés Duque was released.

[74] *My Grandmother*, a Soviet Georgian silent film dating from 1929, directed by Kote Mikaberidze. A spoof of the impossible Soviet bureaucracy, it was banned in the Soviet Union, and the original score was lost, but Oleg Karavaychuk composed a new score when it was re-released in 1976. Most versions of the film now available have a new score by Beth Custer, commissioned by the Berkeley Pacific Film Archive.

The pleasure of an unplanned meeting. Running into people you
know, like bumping into ghosts. A presence you thought had left your
life, or someone you believed was far removed, but whom

> you suddenly find
> sharing the same air.

Like Sam, Anna, or Rebecca Solnit with her signature hat, and hair
under it.

The body disguised as something else entirely. A key, a beat. A
drumhead on which (diluted?) milk dances.

This year, a new association with ashes: a co-worker who couldn't get
off in time to visit her father's ashes on the anniversary of his death.
The ashes and their vessel were in her uncle's possession, all the way
down in San Leandro, or maybe somewhere further south. A five
hour long trip by public transportation. *He'd offered to share them with
me, but I didn't want them to be spread out all over the place, his soul split
up.*"[75]

Groceries I know I got because I photographed them on my phone in
pre-departure nostalgia:

Clover organic whole milk in its red carton. Red, always means whole milk.

A half dozen eggs.

Easter egg radishes.

Grape tomatoes.

Dried dates.

One beet, sans greens.

Three yellow peaches.

One white peach.

Two pears.

Three shallots.

One yellow onion.

One head garlic.

One bunch mint.

One basket of red figs.

One jar of preserved lemons.

One box "organic girl" brand salad greens.

One mystery product, unidentifiably shrouded in
reflective plastic.

It was Ramadan. I'd arrived at the chapel with Ariana but she
had gone earlier, the presence of ghosts being too much. I left with
Patrick[76] as the sun fell. We shared dates and walked with his bike
back to Grant Street, where I was staying. It's easy not to eat, just takes
a little practice.

[75] Truth is, I don't know what to think of the body, its rest, and its relationship to the soul either in life or after death.

[76] A different Patrick from the previous.

Hitched a ride to Runmarö on Bo's[77] motorboat – cigarette boat?
with an American-flag blanket covering the cushion. He'd be going
to Miami in January for a boat show. I'd be going too, for a poetry
conference. Wind molded my face, water and islands blurred in the
cold, gusts teased out tears.

Owner of the bed and breakfast where I'd arranged to stay waited for
me at the dock. He'd written me detailed directions, but I was late and
it was growing dark. He is a psychologist who splits his time between
the city and the isle, and looked the part:[78] plastic frame glasses, navy
blue coat cut close with string-loop buttons. Anders asks, what are you
doing here in September? Quite a lot of stupid people have come to
me since that article came out in the NYT.[79]

I'm on the road to Istanbul.

I hate traveling but I like Istanbul: good bargaining for lamps and
rugs. I hate Muslims.

I'm Muslim.

I was surprised at myself for saying it. You never do know what people
think, who they are, really. I was glad to have spoken up, however
dumbly, but of course he missed the point.

I'm a friendly Muslim
who keeps her hair uncovered,
drinks wine from time to time.

Like that night, when Anders showed me his late-blooming roses (it's very difficult to grow roses which can withstand this cold!) and shared his dinner with me because I'd arrived too late to buy groceries from the one market on the island (and fine thing too, I didn't have enough currency on me and the price of a room was higher than I'd expected, though still very reasonable). I put some petals in my notebook because I thought it would be romantic to send them to Robbie, but I never did send him any physical letters.

"If the lumberjacks don't spend the night, you'll have your pick of cottages."

I preferred the smaller one – cozier, and without wasps[80] bigger than my thumb who crowded around the lamp above the bed.

Fell asleep to Swedish Radio. Classical music, the name Trump interspersed among news commentary in a language I didn't understand.

[77] Swedish was still too unfamiliar for me to decipher his name, so he said, just call me Bo.

[78] Associations with Sweden prior to arrival: IKEA, ABBA, The Cardigans, Lykke Li, Jens Lekman, The Knife, Ingmar Bergman, Force Majeure, Swedish fish, lingonberries, marzipan, meatballs …

[79] It was in fact this article that gave me the idea and excuse to visit the island. I had it in my mind to meet an entomologist, bugs being a side (very far to the side) fascination. In fact, it ended up being very easy to find his house. I asked strangers at the school which resembled a barn, where does the man who studies bugs live? And they pointed me to it. I knocked, but no one was home. So I just peered in the windows, looking for clues.

[80] Later learned they were not wasps, or bees, but hoverflys. In fact, they were the species whom the entomologist was studying. Although they don't sting, they were so loud and large no scientist could have convinced me to sleep peacefully there. Lucky for me, the construction workers didn't show up after all.

RUNMARÖ
September 18, 2015

First time I knew freedom:
On this island,
Awoken with no thought
of anyone, by the coarse beat
of my own heart pounding
in a landscape of its own.

Here I was something unfamiliar, an affront to local magic — a giant
in a forest that was a whole compendium of miniature landscapes.[81]
Fairy-tale sized at first, manageable. With sun and movement I could
shed my jacket, ramble before getting lost: motion de centered by
weather: clouds made me a prowler[82] circling through bushes and
past the same shed in which a witch doll lived, and by the third pass,
grimaced. Folktales came at me, with no guide, no sense of where
aught was:

> water didn't mark West
> or any other direction,[83] shifted
> from placid blue to grey spades.[84]

Stayed a while on the dock at silvertrasket. Lake named not for color,
but for objects of the substance.[85] Not only bodies are buried to haunt[86]
— even the new is haunted by what was there before.[87]

Knew no names, but learned them later from Strindberg[88] and his woodpecker[89] (or was it wood dove?):

> wild rosemary, cotton   grass
> pines, wood pecker – wood dove –
> sedgy meadow,   mountain ash   cypresslike-
> junipers   alder bushes
> (a mountain lake) white birch   water
> lilies   alder trees   reeds
> buckthorn   flytraps

[81] Taken from Strindberg's "The Roofing Ceremony and the Silver Lake"

[82] Wondered what it would take to be mistaken for a prowler in Sweden, where the law permits you (a stranger) to camp on another's property, so long as you accord due respect to the privacy of others. The law does not however specify just how far from someone's window amounts to due respect.

[83] "The way back should have been easy now, when the position of the sun showed the direction home, but the lake was well-guarded, and when his foot sought instinctively the straight patch it did not lean toward the sun, but swung…"

[84] Blind Lemon Jefferson, *See That My Grave is Kept Clean*.

[85] Legend has it that the island's residents sunk their silver in the lake when Russians raided the area in the 18th century. After the danger had passed, they returned to recover their silver but it was impossible to find. Fishermen later reported ghost sightings (but ghosts of what?) so no one fished or built houses around the lake.

[86] "A landscape haunts, intense as opium." –Mallarmé

[87] Walter Benjamin said something about this, but I can't find the quote.

[88] On the island, there were busts of August Strindberg and Tomas Tranströmer, both of whom spent time residing and writing on Runmarö.

[89] "There is a knocking, as at a nighttime door by a latecomer: it is the woodpecker. There is a whimpering and moaning, as of a woman in childbirth: it is the wood dove. He knows all the sounds, he knows all the plants and animals, so that if he heard or saw something unfamiliar, he would take it as an affront."

Even the dead
need room to
breathe and grieve
for their shrinking
Territory.[91]

You can tell a lot by how
people like to be held when dead.[92]

[90] A sparsely populated cemetery with a Scandinavian-style open bell tower. The bell — cast in 1932 by one of Sweden's four remaining clock casters — was beautiful, and I could not resist pulling it.

[91] In Dostoevsky's short story *Bobok*, Ivan Ivanovitch finds a funeral to distract himself from his madness. He sits on a tombstone to think, and suddenly begins to hear the dead below him jostling for room and rank and complaining that one person in particular smells.

[92] People have done every imaginable thing with their bodies and those of their loved ones after death. Bodies have been buried in cars; preserved in glass; smoked; buried in coffins shaped like basketball shoes and pianos; had their skin turned into drum heads, not to mention book covers.

Esteban Patino[94] would like his head thrown down a volcano
after his death.
Just his head.
"There should be an explosion," he says.
You'd better make some good friends while you're alive,
people you can trust

to perform decapitation, trust
to hike up the side of the volcano –
not to mention getting a head through customs alive.
Esteban's birthmark is his grandfather's death.
Grandfather was celebrating Esteban's birth, family legend says,
when he stumbled down stairs and hit his head.

Baby Esteban was asphyxiating until grandfather died from that blow
to his head.
I believe one's soul can pass to another's body, with trust –
that's metempsychosis, Alan says.
Avocados thrive in soil enriched by the ashes of a volcano.
Birth involves a small death.
The mother feels a wrenching pain then boom, you're alive.

You can have anal sex while you're alive.
You can give and get head.
Some men would choose death

over giving head. Giving and getting head takes a lot of trust.
Like walking a friend's head up to the mouth of a volcano.
My friends will do it, Esteban says.

Anal sex makes sense when you're enthralled in another's body,
Esteban also says.
It's best to enjoy your body while it's alive.
Esteban was born in Colombia, where there are 16 volcanoes.
These days Esteban has a bald head.
Esteban makes art these days. Making art takes a lot of trust.
Some say art is a way to delude death.

The French call sex, *la petite mort* –
A thrust exacting the limits of trust –
A boring fact by now, my head says.
It's not too hard, just to stay alive –
The trick is not to lose your head.
Think of yourself as cyclical, like a volcano.

Whether active, dormant, or extinct, a volcano trusts its volcano
nature. No matter what anyone says, no matter what head
someone drops inside: it doesn't mind death, has faith it's alive.

[93] Cremains (cremated remains) can be kept in an urn above a mantle, housed in a columbarium (a memorial building especially designated for cremains), or sprinkled on consecrated ground in a location dear to the dearly departed. Cremains can be scattered to the sea, as in a frequent comedic film or television gag in which the ashes of a loved one blow into the mouths of the living. They can also be shot from a shotgun shell or firework, floated into the air in a helium balloon, or sent into outer space (well, low-earth orbit) temporarily, before they return to our atmosphere. A person's ashes can be compounded into synthetic diamonds, used for portraits and tattoos, or even mixed with cement to create an artificial coral reef that provides a habitat for marine life in a process approved by the EPA.

[94] Atlanta, Georgia-based artist and wordsmith.

DISPOSING OF MY REMAINS

I'd like a pomegranate
tree planted over me
when I die.
I'd like my body
wrapped in white
linen,[95] or placed
in a plain
pine box. A picnic
basket? Rhymes with
casket.

I want people
to eat of me
after my death,
as in life.

I've had a number of offers from lovers
to plant the tree, and tend to it. I guess
they assume I won't outlive them.

My birthmark is red.
I say, Iraq Map. My mother says,
my Heart.

Strangers have said:

Just plain blood.

Lipstick stain.

Felt tip marker.

Paint –

> Once a woman I'd just met licked her finger,
> reached over, and tried
> to rub it off.
> I found that
> endearing.

Lava trickle.

Hickie (since the age of six).

Rocket ship.

Strawberry.

Italy.

Bird.

Shoe.

Heart.

In Arabic, the word for birthmark is *wahma*, stemming from the same
root as 'desire' or 'craving'

        that particularly-womanly –

        Like that which drove the cobbler to steal radishes for his
        gravid wife, resulting in Rapunzel. If her mother's craving
        hadn't been satisfied, Rapunzel (of another name?) would
        have ended up with a radish tattoo somewhere.

Arabic speakers ask me laughingly, did your father not manage to find
some strawberries in time?

From what I can deduce, the true craving was for Home –
stolen and displaced, living where it doesn't belong.

        Last grape on the vine,
        only one of my parents'
        children born in the United States,

but I never answer that way to Strangers.

[95] As in the young cowboy of *Streets of Laredo* fame. In Islam, it is common to enshroud the body in simple white cloth after it has been washed, although particular practices vary across cultures and regions.

After spending about a million hours hatching a million complicated plans, which included taking a train to Bulgaria, Nalini and I, exhausted, stuck to the original:

> *travel to epheSus*
> *by night bus.*

The bus gave us cereal-box surprises. Our ride began with a drive backwards for some hundred meters. Our bus attendant hung out the side of the bus shouting to oncoming traffic. We were given little cups of ice cream, little plastic cups with spoons cleverly attached to the tops. The ice cream was in truth mostly ice, but a welcome cool, welcome melt on the tongue.

Scooping, like shoveling snow
in a sandbox
at age three or so.

The night we left there was a pink moon in a dusky turquoise sky, verging into purple (could I carry these colors in a suitcase?). At a Syrian-owned restaurant near the bus station, they gave us free hummus, salad, baklava. We gave our bread to beggars, and were given more. Nalini said it was because I spoke Arabic, but they didn't seem to recognize me as Arab. Or maybe true recognition's casual. I didn't then realize the extent of the refugee crisis,[96] really, though I would come to that little by little, and then in deep gasps.

On the bus, we were shushed for speaking loudly, giggled and felt very American.

Another night bus surprise: the ferry. At half past midnight, the bus was driven on to cross to the Asian side of Turkey. There was an enclosure of horses: brown and white and quail-egg-speckled. Nalini had watery hot chocolate and toast. I drank horses. They swam throughout the ferry, deck upon deck in my vision, horse rustlings as they nuzzled necks. Wet nose. Horse boat. The moon rose from pink to yellow to gold to cream, and the clouds rushed to meet as it rose up, formed an island city in the water.

[96] This was September 2015. By August 2015, the number of asylum seekers crossing into Europe illegally through Greece and Turkey had more than quintupled since 2014 according to a study by the European Stability Initiative.

SELÇUK, TURKEY

Numb from no sleep, we found our pension and didn't nap but showered quickly and left to make our way to Ephesus.

Saw pomegranate trees and picked their fruit, already splitting. My stomach was on the fritz, so this was one of the few times in my life when I've peeled a pomegranate solely for the pleasure of it. Nal didn't want to eat either, so we just picked at the seeds.

All the women here wore floral printed pants, like the women who worked in the farmlands near my aunt and uncle's place in Yalova[97].

Returning at night, a man followed us back to our pension, to which we nervously found our way back by a business-card map. Looking over our shoulders we whispered to each other, he's still there, he's still there. We tried to ask a group of matronly women if we could walk with them for cover, but couldn't be understood and were merely suspicious. Broke out running, we were all right.

[97] Yalova, Turkey is a city located southeast of Istanbul, about an hour and a half across the Sea of Marmara by ferry boat. Known for its thermal baths, the area is also a major producer of agriculture and flowers.

EPHESUS

Like a dream I half make-up in retelling just after waking:
Dream logic colluding with accepted grammar.

Walking through a "city" that was no longer a city, but did have roads,
rules we break and have no reason to pretend, walking into a closed-
off area thick with blackberry brambles, fig and pomegranate trees
knit together like steel wool.

If you can map it, then
does that make it
functional, or just

legible? One man's legibility is another's scrawl.
Ruin over ruin, but – a city, nonetheless.
After all, it has a name – Ephesus.

And it has a daytime population of tourists and bees – red bees – fuzz
colored like henna, elegant, maybe they were old bees who'd gone to
a salon in preparation for an event; maybe even our arrival. We hop
scotched around them and craned down, fascinated.

In my exhaustion I hallucinated flowers adorning the sloping sides
of the city's walls and, as the sunset fell – an Arcadian sunset, Nalini
named it – I saw a ghost chariot, bony-white and definite, ride across
that orange and neon sky.

Whose myth was it?

Iko-Iko was stuck in my head, from a mix, a gift from Robbie. So there was a drum-stick rhythm to the day.

YALOVA MARKET SEX FANTASY

At the Yalova Market, Khala points out what she'd like and Khalu hands cash and coins to the vendors with their smart collared shirts and showmen's moustaches. Blue and whitish plastic bags catch light when flicked to inhale, shine briefly like lamps, return to us as a measure of lemon or cabbages larger than two of my heads, later to be reincarnated as soup or salad, *murga*[98] to be eaten with rice and bread.

Khala and Khalu have their charade, a practiced dance in which money's passed as if it were a token of something else. I sample olives, heavily-brined cheese, am handed tastes of dry and fresh fruit, and think of you, presence more electric from a distance.

I wanted you then and there, under the market's blue tarps, the material of which, as a child, I thought God was made. I wanted we, invisible but blue-shaded like that God, to fuck on a mat of vegetable scraps and smooshed fruit, to taste each other in nectar-spiked specks of dirt. Our shapes would shift, the surrounding din drift seemingly soundlessly into our rhythm, matching hawkers' calls of tomato, parsley, cucumber. I, covered over, could whimper without fear. Needing a breather, you'd gasp and lay heavy on me like dust-filled light, golden curls wrapped up in mine.

On a coldish day a few months later, we'd be in the same city and I'd tell this fantasy stumblingly to your ear. You'd growl, *get in the car*, drive up the hill and failingly search for a clearing you'd been to two years or more before. As you grew frustrated searching, I'd realize I was beside the point. I liked the light through a tree better than the feeling of you inside and atop me on a slope covered in pine needles, my dress still on so they didn't prick. Better still, climbing into my best friend's bed after, curling up into his warmth and sleeping.

98 General Iraqi term for stew.

SARAJEVO
2015

I think, it's very beautiful –
the graves
how people stop

to pray on their way to work. Unfolding palms by the cemetery fence,
their motion says: opening a book.[99]

It is winter, the cold hangs, caught with the pollution between
mountains. Hills, really.[100]

Like the River[101] in which bluepinkgreen-capped plastic bottles party.

And in the Park,[102] yellow leaves falling as wishes to catch, matching
my stolen sweater, containing all the colors of this world.

There are also graves
here.

But I see a line drawn between memory and mourning.

[99] While saying a quick small prayer (du'a) it is common for Muslims to make a book shape with their hands as they recite.

[100] Sarajevo is nestled between hills, which are themselves situated in a valley of the Dinaric Alps.

[101] The Miljacka River runs through Sarajevo. The city sewage system runs parallel to the Miljacka's flow, and fecal matter sometimes leaks directly into the river. Water treatment plant equipment was looted during the Bosnian War, and the local government is still struggling to meet the expenses necessary to repair the plant and make the river safe for swimming again.

[102] Veliki Park. In which couples grind on each other and make out; in which there is a monument to the Children of Sarajevo who died during the Bosnian war. Sarajevo's central park, it was a cemetery first, in which 16th-century Muslim graves still reside. It is said that burials were forbidden during Austro-Hungarian rule due to sanitation concerns, but some were buried there after the siege of Sarajevo.

SARAJEVO
2015

A place tastes like –

ajvar[103] and eggs, hot pekara[104] – earned warmth, beer

Fog, fog, haze mistaken for fog

Pomegranate syrup we watched a woman bottle
in a side-room, to use for fasanjoon

Ice on grass

> a secret I share with the city,
> since I caught it (almost
> mistook for diamonds or glass)
> on early morning walks
> found a tunnel that was not the famous tunnel[105]
> looked like an old train tunnel – bricked up in
> back, led nowhere; still passageway or shelter:
> shacks with shirts and pants hung, for whom?
> I romanticized[106] empty bottles littering floor and
> "lawn" – maybe an American conceit.

Must romanticizing ruin also mean
romanticizing destruction?

[103] Given to us by Kouros's landlady, Merima, whose face is full of light and who, upon feeling my cold hand, brings a set of long-sleeved pajamas — pink with flowers — down for me. It would be sacrilege to buy ajvar at a supermarket, and wouldn't taste so good besides.

[104] "Bread." Purchased from a window. Put a coin in the portal, receive bread and change.

[105] Sometimes called the Tunnel of Hope, a 25 meter stretch of which is now a museum; when Sarajevo was surrounded by Serb forces from 1992-1995, the tunnel (constructed in 1993 by the Bosnian Army) served as the city's lifeline to the outside world, much as tunnels in Gaza do today. The tunnel ran beneath the airport runway. While it was technically a UN-controlled neutral zone, it was impossible to access the airport safely. The 800 meter tunnel — which was eventually equipped with a railway, allowed Bosniacks to transport food, humanitarian aid, and arms into the city during an international arms embargo and allowed some civilians to flee Sarajevo — including Alija Izetbegovic, then President of Bosnia and Herzegovina. He was carried through the tunnel in a chair, never actually set foot inside it. The tunnel was dug by hand, for 24 hours a day, with workers working in 8 hour shifts from opposite ends. The workers were paid one packet of cigarettes per day, which they could smoke or barter. Regarding the museum's purpose Vladimir Zubić, deputy of the City Council of Sarajevo, noted that the museum is "a reminder of everyone, so that a thing like this tunnel, that provided the people of this city with the minimum subsistence, will never have to be used again. It will be a place where younger people will be able to study a part of our recent past and it will be proof that this part of our history will never be forgotten" https://en.wikipedia.org/wiki/Sarajevo_Tunnel, http://www.nytimes.com/1993/08/15/world/a-crude-1000-yard-tunnel-Is-sarajevo-s-secret-lifeline.html?pagewanted=all&src=pm

[106] I did not know that people had been sprayed down and fired upon in the markets where we picked out fruits for our oatmeal and vegetables for our dinners with a currency we did not yet understand; I could walk in the hills and not know that men had been stationed up there as snipers ... At this time, it did not strike me as significant that my friend lived directly behind a mosque at the foot of these hills, except because we are Muslim.

VRELO BOSNE

Bosnian cousin told me we must go here.

We took the Ilidza[107] train without tickets, paid fines both ways (to the same guard?) because we didn't learn our lesson and stamp our tickets back. No use playing dumb foreigner when you look familiar.

Bought hand-knit socks I could compose an ode to.[108] Kouros offered to hold, then dropped them from under his elbow or armpit.

A woman handed us apple after apple through a fence, which her tree leaned over. Apple bourgeois, so full we could take a single bite and toss the rest into the fields. Detouring accidentally through farm lands. Tufts of hair and later the head of a dead sheep, mostly skull but with a mohawk and some blood left in the figures of bone, filled like pomegranate seeds. Comparison made me sicker.

Walked biked and rode a carriage behind a farting horse at dusk down the tunnel of trees, apparently endless and misty as a runner's dream. No suggestion that this was romantic. Cue the horse farts.

Fog emerged, settled.
A little boy in a red
rain jacket stuck

out from the calm of his farm like a thumb, gathered sheep in for the night.

[107] Ilidza, related perhaps to the Arabic word "iladzge" meaning healing. WWI was triggered by the assassination of Franz Ferdinand in this town.

[108] Always romanticized Neruda's *Ode to My Socks*, and these did remind me of boats or sharks.

I did not write the saints' names.
It was too cold to take my hands,
disguised as hooves, from my gloves.

So, no names of the ones who moved me.[110]

Stared at Rumi's tomb.[111] Felt emotions (not mine)[112] buzzing like flies.

Later, in Miami, I'd ask Miguel Gutierrez[113] what to do about
my heart.

> Have you ever heard of brushing? Move your
> hands or a sponge up and down your body,
> moving away from your heart: Down your legs
> and out from your toes: Up your arms and out
> from your hands: It's like clearing away brush:
> laying a path to the heart.

[109] Following Mongol invasions of Central Asia, Rumi's family left Afghanistan and eventually settled in Konya. This is where Rumi studied, developed Sufism, and gathered his followers. The *tekke*, or school, he founded, remains standing today and his been converted into a museum which houses Rumi's tomb along with those of his father and some of his disciples, a number of fine ancient Qurans, a lock of the prophet Muhammad's beard, and other relics.

[110] There were small chapel-like constructions in which some of Rumi's disciples were interred. I felt connected to a few, a distinct spirit when I entered the room where they were entombed. Later, my friend Norman would suggest that this was a function of architecture; indeed, every structure's construction was unique, and I am a believer in the spirits of buildings ... yet I found myself resisting a solely material explanation for what I had felt.

[111] Engraved with, "do not seek our tombs on this earth, our tombs are in the hearts of the enlightened."

[112] Took photos of strangers crying, appearing reverential, laughing ... Around two million pilgrims visit Rumi's tomb during the annual Mevlana festival, which takes place during the week of his death anniversary (December 17).

[113] Dancer, practitioner of Feldenkrais.

MEVLANA CULTURAL CENTER
Konya[114]

I had traveled to Konya sleep hungry from Istanbul by high-speed
train caught early in the morning. There were screens inside that
indicated in red just how fast the train was going, in kilometers, which
was very thrilling. There was breakfast, tomatoes and olives, cheeses
and honey. There was a beautiful woman across the aisle at whom I
stared for much of the ride, out of the corner of my eye and sometimes
directly.

Early in the train ride, we passed between mountains, mountains
pressing on either side, pressing invisibly because all was obscured
by the densest fog I have ever seen in my life. Soft and purposeful,
sentient even. I cried, overcome by great love –

love that didn't reside
in anything living -
that was, not 'for' or 'to'

but which surrounded, as the fog. Felt beside, above, around myself,
within the fog of God, but not even That – I understood – but not
with the intellect. Belief doesn't leave the body behind.

The cultural center[115] was like a white man in a white suit: hard white,
a clean slate of politics.[116] I was a speck of dust which had been flown
to the wrong planet, words written with the wrong instrument. A
direct answer to the question, how does architecture make you feel? It

existed on an inhuman scale,[117] better described without images, like something designed by Le Corbusier,[118] it was empty, but not like land is empty –

It projected an adult loneliness, and I got out of there as quickly as I could.

English text from an informational placard at the Mevlana Cultural Center:

"Short History of Konya Metropolitan Municipality Mevlana Cultural Centre

The need of a place which could host Rumi lovers coming from all over the world by hearing Rumi's call "Come" has been on agenda of our city and also Turkey through many years. Searching for an indoor place began in 1980s to annually repeat this call of Rumi, which has been going on for an age, in a more beautiful and attractive place. With this aim, Mevlana Culture Centre Project Contest was held in 1990 and the project of Dr. Hasan Sener, professor at Istanbul Technical University, got the first rank among 69 projects. The foundation of the building, in front of which you stand right now, was laid in 1993; however, during the first ten years of the construction, only 10% of the building could be completed. In 2003, during his visit to Konya, the Prime Minister of the Republic of Turkey, H.E. Mr. Recep Tayyip Erdogan demanded that the construction of the building should be completed in a short span of time. Therefore, Konya Metropolitan Municipality took over the construction of the building through the protocol signed with the Ministry of Culture and Toursim of Turkey Republic in 2004. The rest of the construction was completed under the supervision of Konya Metropolitan Municipality in one hundred days thanks to a team of one thousand people working 24/7 despite harsh winter conditions. Mevlana Culture Center was opened by H.E. the Prime Minister Mr. Recep Tayyip Erdogan in 2004. More than 400,000 people can annually benefit from Mevlana Culture Centre for several activities. Mevlana Culture Centre of Konya Metropolitan Municipality is located on the land of 28.255 m^2 within the area of 100.000 m^2. It has an indoor Sama Hall of 3000 people, the largest one in the world, a main entrance and foyer areas of 2.500 m^2, exhibition spaces, Konya and Mevlana Specialty

Libraries, Sultan Veled Hall with a capacity of 600 people and various departments of Konya Metropolitan Municipality. Moreover, there are an indoor Sama Hall and the parking area with 400 car parking capacity. I wish you, visitors and people of Konya, could enjoy this distinguished building which has the capacity to host various activities every day of the year. — Tahir Akyurek Mayor of Konya Metropolitan Municipality"

[115] Where the main Sema occurs, and in which there were vendors selling various Sufi tchotchkes.

[116] Sufism's history is fraught in Turkey. In Ataturk's newly-founded "secular" Turkish Republic, Sufi orders were banned and their institutions were shut down in 1925. Many Sufis emigrated to other parts of the former Ottoman Empire, such as Syria, Albania, and Bosnia, to continue their practices. However, the Mevlavi order (the best-known Sufi order, with whirling dervishes) began to be resuscitated in the mid-1960s when the Turkish government recognized their power as a tourist attraction.

[117] I use the term "inhuman" not as a value judgment, but as a descriptive fact.

[118] Turkey was not left out of Le Corbusier's orientalist architectural dreams. In May 1911, on a visit to the city (but before his arrival there) Le Corbusier wrote of what he imagined Istanbul should be: "I want Stamboul to sit upon her Golden Horn all white, as raw as chalk, and I want light to screech on the surfaces of domes which swell the heap of milky cubes, and minarets thrust upward, and the sky must be blue … Under the bright light, I want a city all white, but the green cypresses must be there to punctuate it. All the blue of the sea shall reflect the blue of the sky."

DOLMENS
Madaba, Jordan[119]

It was the weekend, and we felt we must search for something. We found the dead with a piss-poor map from a hotel where we stopped to ask for directions.

A good feeling to find something by a bad map. To look at rocks and wonder – just rocks? Shelter for the dead? Could any boulder be? Resting-place for giants?

Andrew comments, "You're so small" as I clamber into his truck. I ignore that.

A lucky feeling, to have a truck, to drive far out of the way and loop back. To look for, without being sure, until it is before you and you just know.

Pissed on a grave, which sheltered me cave-like from the wind and my own piss.

[119] Single-chamber megalithic tombs, mostly dating from the early Neolithic age (around 4000-3000 BC). They are made of a few vertical stones which support another that lies flat table-like (or roof-like) across them.

CHELLAH
Rabat, Morocco[120]

"This statue has no ass,
it's what we call a flattie
in the biz."[121]

I always hated skirts whose pleats or print did not carry
to the back. It always felt a little cheap and (I'll give
them) – sly.

[120] Referred to as a Necropolis, though it was at various points a home for the living as well as for the dead. Today, storks nest there and human beings just pass through.

[121] The words of Dr. James Miller, not mine.

IBN BATTUTA'S TOMB
Tangier, Morocco

Ibn Battuta's tomb is closed, and we haven't a phone to call the number of its attendant, so we incant and crumble cookies a man gave me at the mosque the night before into the crevices around the doorframe. Bless us on our travels, we ask, and are blessed.

Arturo said, my name's Arthur, I liked your song that said "shoebox
full of spit," I wish I could've heard the rest of the words.

I said, Arthur, like Arthur Rimbaud, do you like poetry too?

He said, I like that, people always say King Arthur, Rimbaud's better.

Only positive associations with Arthurs so far:

———— Rimbaud,

King ———— Flour, my family's preferred brand
for some unknown reason

———— the Aardvark, from the PBS cartoon

———— Russell

and now ———— Wieczorkiewicz.

It's Polish, he said.
Can you spell it?

Arthur wrote his full name down along
with his number in my phone.

I can search it now, months after you died, and I'm too shy to ask anyone how and bring up the pain. I found out it through Instagram, and stood sad stunned in my living room, in Amman. Didn't cry till hours later, when I realized the upstairs neighbor's toilet had leaked and flooded my hallway. How quickly the moisture bent my books. I can listen to all the videos you liked on YouTube six years ago. Buena Vista Social Club, Marcel Khalife.[123] I get with your rhythm. I can see the few texts we sent in Summer 2016, I was reading Rimbaud in your honor, and Robert Browning. You were reading Bob Dylan and Shel Silverstein. Clearly superior choices. Though Bob does mention Arthur[124] so maybe we weren't too far from each other there.

> June 27, 2016: Hey Noor! Have you ever been to the pub on Solano in Albany? Awesome space to think and have conversations Also I work from 330-830 today so if you're free …"

We missed each other.

> "Saul is goodman/hopefully another day"

> "Egg ate it now" to save face after missing your pun, self-conscious about canceling on you.

We didn't go together, but I did make it to the pub at ten p.m. or so. I got a coffee. Don't remember what I was reading that day. Don't think I liked it instantly. I think it was, You Too Can Have a Body Like Mine. An old man was reading something on a tablet. He spoke to me because I was reading on paper. That's rare, he said. I see the humor in it better now. He translated Rilke for fun, to practice his German. We talked about a poem he was translating, I remember it had to do with a tiger. I'd just gotten a copy of *The Notebooks of Malte Laurids Brigge*. This guy said he kept a favorite passage from it on his person at all times. I was expecting a yellowed paper in his pocket, but it was on his phone, cloudshare. He read it to me.

The next time I went, also alone for some reason, I had coffee and a clove cigarette. It was my first cigarette. I didn't know you had to suck in while lighting it. I was stressed, I knew I'd be leaving this place, the Bay, home, behind, and had no clue for how long. The cigarette unintentionally signaled permanent change. A first time opening the door to a second, or a lifetime of habit. The not-knowing made me sick and sad and speechless, except with strangers. Like this guy Gabriel, a farmer who was in town for his twin brother's wedding to a girl he didn't much approve of. We talked about Isaac Babel, and went out dancing the next night. He leaned his bike along a wooden fence while we kissed. Some plant we'd picked and put in his pocket smelled like kindergarten. I hadn't any conscious memory of what kindergarten smelled like till then.

You and I never met at the Albany Pub or anywhere else after that first time.

I see a picture of you on your CouchSurfing profile, and want to cry. We spoke for maybe ten minutes. I've never been to the countries you've visited, except California. I thought you were one of those people who would be a great friend, given the right time and geography. I still do think so.

You were right. Albany Pub: awesome space to think and have conversations.

[122] Its true name is Schmidt's Pub.

[123] The title of the Khalife song translates to, "The Most Beautiful Memories." Also on the list – Lil B, Antonio Carlos Jobim ...

[124] "Situations have ended sad, relationships have all been bad, mine've been like Verlaine's and Rimbaud," he sings in You're Gonna Make Me Lonesome When You Go

SARAJEVO
2017

A brighter season now, though perhaps just as cold – the contrast between the living and the dead, tighter drawn, and now I speak to someone and dreams are evident.

VIŠEGRAD
Bosnia

A birthday destination recommended to us by a sushi chef and
saxophone player.

Still in Bosnia, but divided by the Serbian border.

Like a beach town accidentally built on a riverbank, then abandoned
– like Bombay Beach in California, another fake. At least this water
moves, thinks.

We stayed in a barn-shaped hotel with a seedy-looking owner – he
looked like an actor playing a car salesman. The room smelled like the
pension near Ephesus, chemical.

Seen in light the morning after:
Sunday morning, after fish
from the Drina washed
down with beer after beer and red light –

The church found by following the invisible air-
trails of parishioners finished with worship, making their way down a
winding path.

Before the church are the graves – slabs of black stone, shiny black,[125]
with words and images carved in – they are all soldiers. I do not wish
to take a picture of this.

On the front side of each grave stone, the boy's face – full body
rendered on the back –
He is not portrayed any handsomer on stone than he was alive.[126]

Half a city in a city
(pick a penny, what a penny –)
no kids to skip rope

Why we even entered the church, I don't know. It seemed right, in a
way, but wasn't.
I joked, should we sip wine and wafers, blood and body
But we were too sad – stunned and I
Guess we didn't really want to be part of this body –

[125] Such a contrast to the Muslim graves in Bosnia and Turkey – white with rounded tops. This style of grave markers are represented by the headpieces worn by Mevlevi Sufi dervishes, a woman at a dargah I visited in Konya told me – tall and white, with rounded tops – they symbolize life's revolution around death. Through their whirling practice, the dervishes are in a sense spin-driving themselves into their graves. Death is often seen as the meeting place with God in Islamic theology; hence preparations for the Hajj journey to Mecca are like preparations for death (paying back debts, setting one's affairs in order).

[126] Great sculptors who have had to become gravestone carvers in life under fascist regimes are a theme in art and literature. There's the art teacher in Croatian writer Josip Novakovich's story "Rust" – "Since in a poor socialist society nobody could afford sculptures except for the Communist government, and he no longer wished to work for them, Marko Kovachevich could not make a living as a sculptor. He became a tombstone-maker, specializing in the tombstones of deceased Party members." Then, there's Georgian director Eldar Shengelaia's film "An Unusual Exhibition" about a sculptor who, returning from soldier-hood, uses his skill to carve tombstones bearing likenesses of the dead. He's saving one block of marble for a very special project.

PASHUPATINATH

Rich man, poor man: sandalwood, teak[127]: a higher price for a more fragrant pyre: Pashupatinath. I decline a tour, sit at the edge of things and watch men stoking, sweat. Railroad work. A dog begs. I am not interested in "being strong." A man approaches me and sits beside, pointing: Ma ma ma ma ma mama – That's my mo – mo – mo – Mother – my mother is dead.

> He points at a fire,
> second from the left
> on the teak side of the
> river.

> > A fire, a pyre,[128] a
> > burning mother – a burning
> > bush couldn't dream of being so pure –
> > by the Bagmati[129] –
> > Pani means water

I consider dipping my hands in the river, but these aren't my dead.[130]

Ma ma ma – my mama ma mo mo mo – mother –

> He had traveled from South Korea to burn his
> mother's body.

What's the proper term?

Go back and forth in your head, and "burn" sounds no more violent than "bury."

Pyres are maintained by stoking the flame and raking the pyre to allow good oxygen flow – a continuation, breathing.

Associations with burning:

Becoming gas
and ash
mineral fragments – alternate bone

Can't genetically sequence ash. Can genetically sequence a wooly mammoth. Can't genetically sequence Trotsky, who was cremated.

A death is fertile, fertility we associate with soil – but ash can be that. I reference avocados, and their preference (yes, a fruit prefers) for volcanic ash-enriched soil –

Fertility exists beyond DNA and its ability to repopulate, cut and paste.

The man whose mother had died (did I ever learn his name?) bought me tea from a sadhu who lounged sexy in his orange cloth and ash. I bought an extra bottle of water for him, and he seemed upset – why did I get something separate?

Eventually I left the man who was watching his mother, and wandered through the temple grounds.[131] A man had been sitting across from me, holding a black plastic bag, watching. He followed me far up steps, through the grounds. I sat by a braided tree, human roots, to look around. At a monkey milking its young. A wedding party taking photographs and eating snacks wrapped in cones of newspaper.

The plastic bag man winked and I was not so much scared, as annoyed by silent incursion upon my silence. Contemplation turned affect.

[127] When I visited the cost was 10,000 rps (~100 USD) for a poor man's teak-wood funeral, and 20,000 rps (~200 USD) for a rich man's sandalwood cremation. The cost of a ticket in was 1,000 rps – a tenth of a death. Tourists could fund the funerals of all Nepal, if only they weren't so scared of dying themselves.

[128] In the Wikipedia entry on Pyres there is a single line about Hindus, Sikhs, and other South Asian practitioners of cremation. Anthropologists have been able to track the advance of Christianity throughout Europe with the appearance of cemeteries. By the 5th century, with the spread of Christianity, the practice of burning bodies gradually disappeared from Europe.

[129] The source of Nepalese civilization and urbanization, the river is holy to both Buddhists and Hindus and draws the border between Patan and Kathmandu.

[130] Not so common nowadays as it once was, but following a cremation, many relatives from a funeral procession take a bath in the Bagmati or sprinkle its water on their bodies. It is believed that the Bagmati's water purifies people spiritually.

[131] Pashupatinath is a Hindu temple (although Buddhists also pray, cremate their dead, and go to die there) complex about 1.7 km^2 in area. While the complex is open to visitors, only Hindus may enter and worship in the temples themselves.

A SHOPPING CENTER, BUT REALLY JUST A PARKING LOT, ARLINGTON AVENUE BETWEEN ARDMORE AND BOYNTON

It's dark and we pass a spook on the way — a doll with stringy purple hair hanging from a tree, A MENACE ON A PUBLIC STREET!

Don't know what we're looking for and I trawl about for a thing, follow a ramp up and drag in a whole parking lot on the roof of a building that looks like it couldn't bear it if any cars actually parked there. There's a white spray paint scrawl of *I love you* and a heart drawn clumsy and swelling.

Try to imagine someone gesturing romantically here, and fall over doing. There could be a great view, I don't know. It's too open for any echoes, games with spooks, ethereal conjurings. From here it looks like just

another city of rooftops
all their vents stuck up
and puffing.

GREAT STONE FACE PARK
Thousand Oaks Neighborhood[132], North Berkeley

Rock we sat on,
an unexplained urn[133]
minds me of other
unexplained urns[134]

With the gnarls of coastal live oaks over our heads, the big rock was
an easy climb, even in the dark – purchase simple after months of
practice at climbing trees with Jefferson, who's scared of heights, a fact
I often forget.[135] On another night pilgrimage we'd climbed a tall fir
till we couldn't see the ground, its branches slippery and still as stone.
His head lamp did no good but to serve as a nearer moon and catch
water drops as starry glints. He wasn't scared as I was of my own feet;
he is more worried by the falter of machines. And these watery glints
couldn't be caught in glass.

[132] There's also a Thousand Oaks neighborhood near my hometown, but I don't think there were ever oak trees there.

[133] On the City of Berkeley's web page about Great Stone Face Park, the urn is not even mentioned as a feature. Multi-purpose turf (as if any sort of turf were surrounded by a force field limiting its uses) was deemed more important, apparently. The urn was placed in the early 1900s and actually predates the park. There were at least twenty urns installed throughout the Thousand Oaks neighborhood at that time, and the local neighborhood association raised money in 2011 to restore this particular urn to its former glory, as well as to cast two new urns to join it in the park. The ancient-looking urns are merely ornamental.

[134] The many urns flanking the columns at the Palace of Fine Arts, in San Francisco.

[135] I once forced him into a great glass elevator at the Hyatt hotel in downtown San Francisco, to see the Christmas display. I had seen it the year before when I accidentally joined a gay men's biking group and it had been pure magic – cascades of light fell dramatically as we rose up in the elevator and came down. But, after letting me cajole him into the machine, Jefferson had a near panic attack and I felt very badly about it.

MARIN CIRCLE FOUNTAIN[136]
Thousand Oaks Neighborhood, North Berkeley

Found a stack of New Yorker Magazines and stashed them in my backpack, then left half on a bench,[137] a random half, and I'd trash the others later as I'd read them already.

I remembered the fountain from a dream. I had the dream before I first saw it on a walk a week or so before this sighting. Recognized it immediately and was cast back into the dream-world straight away. In the dream I was all turned around, having passed it on the wrong bus, or rather a bus that had gone the wrong way, wound around[138] and past the fountain and down one of the spokes to a wrong town, unrecognizable although bright and hilly and green.

The dream-fountain was not a solid thing, but the light it cast, that danced on stone. I didn't have the chance to dip my feet in then, so I did now,[139] and danced in front of the un-boned ghosts of the unbuilt capital.

[136] The fountain was the City of Berkeley's first public work of art, and the symbol of an entrance to a great capital city that was never built. In 1908, local developer John Spring (who owned a vast scheme of properties between Grizzly Peak and the Bay) began his campaign to turn Berkeley into California's capital city. The circle (for trains back then) and fountain were meant to mark the grand entrance to the capitol building there. Although the California legislature passed the proposal to move the capital and the governor signed Spring's bill, liquor lobbyists were more powerful, and managed to convince voters to beat the bill proposing the move.

[137] A note from the Friends of the Fountain and Walk, who were instrumental in restoring the fountain: *While we do not encourage the public to walk out to the fountain due to the traffic (there are benches around the perimeter), it is a popular spot for photographs of wedding parties and other special occasions. Also, artists are drawn to the fountain to reproduce it in the form of sketches, pastels and watercolors. When volunteers are maintaining the fountain, motorists driving around the fountain will often shout how much they appreciate the fountain and the work of all the volunteers.*

[138] The fountain is at the center of a roundabout with six spokes (like those that protrude from the center of any decent capital city) emerging from it.

[139] The Friends of the Fountain and Walk are not merely being nosy neighbors when they discourage cavorting in the fountain: there have been accidents in the confusing roundabout, around which many steep streets loop. In 1958, an errant truck sped down Marin Avenue, rammed into the fountain, and broke it beyond repair. It was not restored until 1994.